BORN FROM SILENCE

BORN FROM SILENCE

MARK ANTHONY GRUBB

Born from Silence

Published by
Inscript Publishing
a division of Dove Christian Publishers
P.O. Box 611
Bladensburg, MD 20710-0611
www.inscriptpublishing.com

All poems and quotes
copyright © 2018 by Mark Anthony Grubb

Cover Design by Mark Yearnings

All rights reserved. No part of this publication may be used or reproduced without permission of the publisher, except for brief quotes for scholarly use, reviews or articles.

Library of Congress Control Number: 2018909845

ISBN: 9781732112520

Printed in the United States of America

DEDICATION

I dedicate this book first of all to the glory of my Almighty God and to my Lord & Savior Jesus Christ, who has been the voice out of silence that has persuaded me to write most of the words you will read. In the stillness and darkness of night, even when my shadow abandons me, he is always with me.

I also dedicate this book to my loving wife Rocio for her encouragement to fulfil an unspoken promise. To my late mother Ruby, who was my first human contact, the first woman I loved, the one who soothed me on restless late night watches and, above all, for being my spiritual rock and the still waters that gave me sanctuary in the depth of God's word.

To everyone who reads these words I hope you will be lifted up by the same Holy Spirit and by the word that comes with an urgent sense of time. It is my hope and prayer that this little light of mine will shine strong enough so that you will be filled with the joy and reflection that comes from knowing the great I Am and the fullness of his love, his mercy and his grace.

CONTENTS

Dedication	v
Your Shadow	3
Ageless Albums	4
There Isn't Anymore	6
God's Fresh Fire	7
Thank You Mom	8
The Shadow of The Cross	9
Tears Upon The Web	10
Empty Manger	12
Small Impressions	14
For One Day Only	17
Before Time Was A Day	18
Falling from Grace	19
Hand Prints Made of Stone	20
This Human Experience	21
Lost	22
Second Chance	23
Isolated	25
The Guardian	26
Remembering	28
Rate of Exchange	29
How?	30
The Essence of Love	31
Swinging Bridge	33
Flying Toward Eden	34
If We Were One	35
Fading Faith	36
All of God's Children	37
Rendezvous	38
The Man I Might Have Been	41
Fallen Leaves	42
The Legend Of The Weeping Willow	44
I Am Grateful	46
I Never Told Brother	47

Denial	48
Invisible Paths	50
Bible of Roses	52
Brief Explanations	53
Soul Survivors	54
The Promise	55
Phenomenon	56
The Masterpiece	57
And God Created Dogs	59
The First Time	60
The Devil Comes To Play	61
The Sea of Life	62
Vacancy	64
Suspended by Wood	65
I Won't Recall	66
The Living Word	67
The Price of Time	69
Who Will Fold The Flag For You	70
Heart to Heart	72
Fade Away	73
The Mist	74
Peace on The Wing	77
Beyond My Blindness	78
Midnight Performance	80
Millers Pond	82
The Sand Dollar	84
School Spirits	86
Time Is on The Wing	87
If I Could Fly	88
Love Found A Way	91
Children of The Storm	92
Borrowed Body	94
If All We Had Was Us	95
How Could We Know	96
The Street Named Forever	97
Six Hours to Paradise	98

The Song	99
Did You Ever Laugh?	101
Nemesis	102
A Look Inside	103
The Promise	104
The Trespasser	105
Just For Me	106
Bone by Bone	107

"When you have giants standing in front of you just remember your deliverance is only a stone's throw away." ~ Mark Anthony Grubb

YOUR SHADOW

The sun no longer casts your shadow long,
Angels have taken you and now you're gone.
No matter how long life is short and brief,
Full of some laughter and a measure of grief.

The cross you were nailed to for us has remained,
In the hearts that love you and call on your name.
The shadow of God's son the seed Mary would bear
Lead us to eternal life and the power of prayer.

The cross is the symbol of suffering and shame
You said not a word and you took all of the blame.
Your shadow now altered by a crown full of thorns
This babe in a manger for this moment was born.

You taught us life isn't measured by number of years
Nor struggles and suffering and yielding of tears.
It's measured by those we have loved in this life,
And by those we have lead to you Jesus Christ.

AGELESS ALBUMS

Reflections in a shutter
Suspended within time.
Eternal pose of memories
In pictures that I find.

Silent and unmoving caught
Ageless in a frame.
Some faces are familiar
Yet others without names.

Presents from another time
A Christmas long ago.
Eyes beaming with excitement
And faces all aglow.

Antique timeworn memories are
Etched on every page.
This album captures actors
Appearing on life's stage.

Curtain call comes swiftly and
We will take our place.
We'll rest in ageless albums
With our smiling timeless face.

THERE ISN'T ANYMORE

Time runs out and everyone that you love and adore,
Will suddenly be gone and won't be back anymore.
No more laughter and crying, no more lingering hugs,
No phone calls or flowers from the one that you love.

No more movies to watch or special secrets to share,
Plans must be cancelled since someone's not there.
You'll make new discoveries as you prowl and explore,
Finding pictures of loved ones you can't hold anymore.

Memories come to mind with every song that you hear
You'll slow dance with those that you long to have near.
In your dreams you'll laugh with those you loved before,
Then you will wake up to find they're not here anymore.

Live your life by loving and laughing not shedding tears,
Remembered in others hearts with the passing of years.
Be a stranger to regret and to the heavens fly and soar,
When your time here is finished and there isn't anymore.

GOD'S FRESH FIRE

The prophecy of the messiah
Mary's baby time has come.
The man of many sorrows
God's only begotten son.

Satan mocked God's selection
The word would be his foe.
The begotten of God almighty
In his image from head to toe.

The lame begin to walk anew
The blind begin to see.
The grip of death was broken
By God's fresh fire and seed.

The end of days is coming
Says the mighty Lord of hosts.
A portal bursts in heaven
Pouring out the Holy Ghost.

A blood red burst of glory
Flows from a chosen son.
Satan's head is wounded
When Jesus said it's done.

Fresh fire burns like a cinder
The church spawns its rebirth
The last call from the living God
To his children here on earth.

THANK YOU MOM

Thank you mom for your watchful eyes,
For the rocking chair and lullabies.
For your legs before I could walk,
And for your words before I could talk.

Thank you mom for teaching me to pray,
For reaching out when I did stray.
For kisses you placed on my tiny cheeks,
And for your protection when I was weak.

Thank you from for the tears you shed,
For being my hands when I was fed.
For being my friend on sleepless nights,
And for being my eyes before I had sight.

Thank you Mom for tucking me into bed,
For understanding things I did and said.
For denying yourself so that you could give,
And for dying a little so I might live.

THE SHADOW OF THE CROSS

The church persecuted and Christians abhorred,
Despised for their worship and praise of the Lord.
One nation divided, separation of states,
Everyone has the right to love or to hate.

Who'll embrace the hero's that have no arms
That can no longer defend or keep us from harm?
Who'll will hit their knees to cry for mercy and grace
To our Lord from which we have hidden our face?

The silent majority has vanished away,
Complacent Americans have nothing to say.
Harbingers tell lies to a world that is lost,
Truth is still standing in the shadow of the cross.

Our spiritual liberty and creeds are falling apart,
Men guided by greed and not by their hearts.
Old Glory is hated and church pews are bare,
The light of the world is simply not there.

We the people continue to elect and defend,
The masters of illusion and the champions of sin.
This nation of hero's this home of the brave,
Souls in the wind of forever just drifting away.

TEARS UPON THE WEB

The forest is ominous on this misty summer mourn,
Stretched across the pathway a spider's web is born.
Within its silky structure I see the woven beds,
And morning mist is hanging like tears upon the web.

I despised the spider that hung this vulgar snare,
While victims hang suspended upon this humid air.
Vibrations of thrashing wings sing out in earnest pleas,
The Butterflies are weeping, their only hope is me.

I glared upon my target my aim it mustn't miss;
I will save the helpless from the fatal spiders kiss.
Then my swing was halted and crumbled to my side,
I questioned my intervention, of just who lived or died.

I submitted to the powers that rule the forest depths,
Nature was the victor, as I looked on and wept.
My tiny little creatures like us had gone astray;
We all become entangled, when we have lost our way.

Hung upon the web of life unyielding to the powers,
We're searching for our destiny in every waking hour.
But when the searching's over we'll hang our muddled heads,
And find our life was nothing, but tears upon the web.

EMPTY MANGER

Where is this precious baby boy
That once here laid his head?
His name I hear was Jesus
And once this was his bed.

You say this baby named Jesus
Was born to die for me?
The child born in this manger
Would die to set men free?

This is not a proper bed,
This trough where cattle fed.
He deserved the best I cried,
To lay his sacred head.

Then my dream was finished,
As tears fell on my bed.
To think this tiny infant,
Hung on the cross and bled.

I long to hold that baby boy,
Who died for me a stranger.
But all that's left of sacrifice,
Is a humble empty manger.

SMALL IMPRESSIONS

I watched the little children
That molded sea washed sand.
Watching pure creation take
Form from baby hands.

The fashioned twinkling Camelot's
From minds as pure as snow.
While leaving small impressions
Of tiny hands and toes.

I laughed at their insistence
To conquer crashing waves.
They giggled and they chuckled
Like me in younger days.

The call from mother signaled
That they would have to leave.
Their tiny faces saddened
As they looked out to sea.

As footprints and handprints faded
And castles fell apart.
The sea will never wash away
Their impressions on my heart.

"The nest is never empty though they leave me one by one. They never leave my presence for my heart is what they won." ~Mark Anthony Grubb

FOR ONE DAY ONLY

If today was your last then what would you change?
With twenty four hours being all that remains.
Would the sky look different its texture and hue?
Will everything you see look different and new?

Would you spend time praying for those left behind?
What in this world would be the last on your mind?
Is all well with your soul or perhaps you have doubt
For one day only you can change things about.

No more wishing the weeks and the days all away
You'll plead for the seconds and minutes to stay.
A lifetime of memories will race through your head
Remembering every good and bad thing you said.

The great and the small will be equal at last
The former things gone no future nor past.
Forever has never been this close in your life
The only thing important is the Lord Jesus Christ.

BEFORE TIME WAS A DAY

In my quite times I have a rendezvous,
A roll call with friends both old and new.
I recall memories both bitter and sweet
Remembering the promises I failed to keep.

I recall mistakes and the resulting pain,
The smell of the air after a summer's rain.
The miracle of birth from nature's womb,
The late night watches of despair and gloom.

I recall kittens and the beauty of pups,
Foes I have conquered with incredible luck.
The excitement that surged first driving a car,
The grandeur and splendor of each tiny star.

I recall the tenderness of an innocent kiss,
The pain of rejection and the wonder of bliss.
The awe I feel as I look upward toward space
It is there that God has reserved me a place.

I recall laughter and singing God's praise,
A spiritual awakening in innocent days.
My soul has a memory yet it's faded away,
A cobweb existence before time was a day.

FALLING FROM GRACE

Don't follow the crowd and those that are blind,
Satan is their father and he'll feed you a line.
He'll fill your head with false hope and illusion,
He is the father of all liars and total confusion.

He's the king of all misery and father of death,
And if you allow it he'll take your last breath.
When you forsake Jesus then he takes control,
Then he takes possession of your mortal soul.

When your body is tired and you're needing rest,
Demons will come calling and put you to the test.
Who will care for your soul but the king of kings?
Your first love, your companion, your everything.

Who broke your chains and gave you salvation?
Who died for the world and bled for all nations?
Who hears your prayer when you're in despair?
The name above all others is the one that cares.

The sky is the limit for that's as far as you go,
Your reward is not in heaven it's here below.
Your soul is drifting toward a tormented place,
Take the Lords hand you are falling from grace.

HAND PRINTS MADE OF STONE

I see your tiny hand prints here engraved in stone,
In a cracking sidewalk that use to lead to home.
These baby hands and fingers don't even give a clue,
No name was left behind but I know that it was you.

You left your mark here in your rural walk of fame,
Proof that you existed now fades from years of rain.
Your impression is all faded but you are not erased,
Existence is persisting where tiny hands were placed.

Hand prints made of stone is not all you left behind,
You linger in our memory our hearts and in our minds.
Your spirit carved impressions with your love and grace,
We feel your joyful presence that doesn't need a face.

THIS HUMAN EXPERIENCE

We search for life's meaning and why that we are here,
A child of God in transit now clothed with flesh and fear.
This human experience we're living, it is a test of God,
To see which sheep are faithful and guided by his rod.

Souls restlessly waiting as babes underneath his wings,
God's spiritual creatures that wait to speak and sing.
Waiting for the beam of light as God sits on his throne,
A sea of souls drifts toward earth our temporary home.

Our soul takes on the likeness of a woman or a man,
Born in God's own image and the purpose of his plan.
A wonder of creation born as heaven shouts with joy,
Children of the living God become tiny girls and boys.

Innocent and helpless and born so blind and small,
Satan aware of each arrival plans to make us fall.
But babes cannot be tempted, this we can be sure,
For sin cannot win over a heart so clean and pure.

Eternal souls now battle with temptations of mere man,
Unruly children of free will with moving arms and hands.
Flesh is frail to sins of choice and ears refuse to hear,
God's distant voice is calling as the end of time is near.

LOST

I was so lost and lonely my soul was brought to test
The master I was serving he gave no peace or rest.
My faith had all but faded the world became my friend
I was chained and shackled by the burden of my sins.

In despair I said the sinner's prayer like I was told to do
It didn't work for me dear Lord I wasn't getting through.
I left the walking dead behind to find the gospel truth
I studied man made doctrines and all were lacking proof.

I never stood in front of men and your name confessed
I made some bad decisions my choices weren't the best.
I made a few small changes but never changed my ways
You said repent or perish and time counts down my days.

I believe you are the son of God a thief was heard to say
That confession saved him then but your will is law today.
Your revelation show us all how we can reach your blood
Baptism is the bridge to reach your holy crimson flood.

Lord there is strange fire here and worship stranger still
All men claim to worship you but few that do your will.
Satan has deceived the nations with all his twisted lies
He leads your sheep astray Lord a shepherd in disguise.

SECOND CHANCE

I want a second chance to live,
To give more than I took.
I don't want to live but once,
Please grant a second look.

I want a second chance to be,
Everything I knew I could.
A chance to be a brand new me,
To be equal and understood.

I want a second chance to sing,
The songs my heart embraced.
To say goodbye forever is sad,
And disappear without a trace.

I want a second chance at life,
I want to clean my slate.
I want a pardon for myself,
And all my past mistakes.

I want a second chance to love,
Like I never loved before.
I want a second chance to see,
What I had missed before.

"A Life without God is like music without the lyrics. Your soul has nothing to sing about." ~Mark Anthony Grubb

ISOLATED

Oh Lord the world is heating up
No escape from lashing flames.
Everyone is mocking Christians
And those that wear your name.

I'm lifting up my heart and hands
Have mercy Lord I'm just a man.
The world is busy throwing stones
Sometimes I feel like I'm alone.

May I find the path not often walked
The narrow one that others mock.
Let me feel no pride and humbly live
May I give you all that I can give.

I pray for strength to walk by faith
To pray for those who thrive on hate.
A sound mind that is not confused
So I may know just what to do.

THE GUARDIAN

We are like the spewing mist
Human waves on restless seas.
The power of a living ghost,
That dwells in you and me.

Souls sent down from glory
We arrive in babies forms.
A mother's womb houses us
Until we are all transformed.

Two stages of existence
The same yet they're apart.
One dwells in our emotions,
The other in our hearts.

One will fail and one lives on
One is frail and one is strong.
The soul is the breath of God
And to the almighty it belongs.

The guardian of our existence
That waits for a trump to blow.
The soul waits for the reunion
With its image on earth below.

REMEMBERING

I trace my life
And reminisce.
Images of peace
And relationships.

Memories made
Reserved in me.
Time will not yet
Set them free.

Total recall of
People and things.
Tender moments
And tears that sting.

Springs that we
Prayed would last.
Still live with me
In youth gone past.

All that is left is
Just some history.
The vagueness of life
That's just a mystery.

RATE OF EXCHANGE

God's word rejected in the fire it's hurled,
So hard to find truth in our secular world.
Whether falling apart or falling in place,
God has given all of his mercy and grace.

Serving the savior the world has forgot,
Nothing is random as we cast our lots.
Women in labor give life with a scream,
Mother and child push to their extremes.

The clock of life runs its programmed course,
While masses are in denial without remorse.
The center will not hold nor will it restrain,
As life crumbles from the rate of exchange.

We start drawing from the bank of time,
So busy spending it to notice the signs.
Time has an awesome rate of exchange,
Youth's soon attached to a ball and chain.

HOW?

How can a soul feel pain when it can't heal?
How can a soul react to flesh and living will?
How could I cling to life before I could hold?
Are all my emotions connected to my soul?

How can I be one yet two close but far apart?
One living by logic and one lives by the heart.
How can my soul have eyes that will never cry?
How can my soul live without me and never die?

How will my soul bow on legs that have no bones?
When on my knees in judgment I will stand alone?
How will my soul forget yet remember who I am?
How will it find me among God's countless lambs?

THE ESSENCE OF LOVE

Love is an attraction and it is for real,
The pulse of emotion that all of us feel.
First felt as babes when we are young,
A joy we cannot speak with our tongues.

Love is our center from where it gives.
Life with a purpose and reason to live.
Hope above hope in the bosom of us,
Sanctuary of God and a feeling of trust.

The heart of love is a mist of wonder,
A gentle lamb and a roar of thunder.
Loss without equal when it disappears,
Silence is shattered by crying and tears.

Prodigy of God no beginning or end,
Core of creation and free of all sin.
It can't be measured or put on a scale,
Yet love was hung by three rusty nails.

"We were not born for the moment; the moment was born for us." ~ Mark Anthony Grubb

SWINGING BRIDGE

Life is a swinging bridge we walk each day,
We walk in our sleep trying to find our way.
We pitch and sway and don't hear the sound,
The footfalls of evil as it's running around.

My mind sends new words to renew and relate,
The nectar of wisdom that speaks of our fate.
Gandhi is not needed to direct how it's done,
To see how our shadows all flirt with the sun.

We must look past the folly of our intentions,
Pride and contempt and all our inventions.
We are so afraid of death we forget to live,
On the verge of forever yet never forgive.

FLYING TOWARD EDEN

Taking to flight drawn by an invisible beacon and force
We do not fly blinded we have all chose a course.
Bright chariots of fire exposing the greens & grays
We appear flashing brightly and then fade away.

We fly on smoke signals in the mist of the night
As winds of uncertainty blows with all of its might.
Soaring toward Eden on a wing and a prayer
Faith is our road map and we hope it's still there.

Lovers and crickets serenade the moon as it glows
The God of creation is watching us all here below.
He sees every flutter as we fly frantically about,
He searches the faithful and those who have doubt.

We flicker like lightning bugs broadcasting our light,
Our life shimmers brightly with wrong or the right.
With each flash of light we display life and endeavors,
Knowing that the light of our life will not shine forever.

IF WE WERE ONE

Since we are all of one blood it's hard to see,
Why we can't get along just you and me.
We're so much alike we have joys and fear,
Yet we can't agree on what we say or hear.
If we were one we would not have confusion,
We would see eye to eye without any illusion.
We'd build upon love instead of tearing apart,
The foundation of joy that dwells in the heart.
If we were one then hate could not thrive,
If we loved one another it couldn't survive.
Forgiveness would flourish and never die,
If we were all one we would give it a try.
If we were one we'd see right from the wrong,
Poor would be equal to the rich and the strong.
If we were one then the Lord would expand,
The mansions in heaven he's building for man.

FADING FAITH

When you feel lost and off your pace,
And you feel rejected and void of grace.
When your faith has all but disappeared,
Remember God loves you and he still hears.

Moving forward the world seems strange,
To children of God having growing pains.
We will stumble and fall and sometimes cry,
But the word of God soothes like a lullaby.

Trust he is working everything to your good,
Stand when you've done everything you could.
Remember we walk by faith and not by sight,
So believe with your heart and all of your might.

This world is full of misery and rich in despair,
But God will stand with you when nobody cares.
Don't lose hope and let your faith not waiver,
Just lean upon Jesus, your Lord and your Savior.

ALL OF GOD'S CHILDREN

Looking around our house I see deprivation,
The love on our lips is just a desecration.
Love for one another cannot be disguised,
Love cannot be silent nor does it hide.

Jesus said we should love one another,
Our family in Christ our sisters and brothers.
If one in our family has suffering or need,
Then we should help them by action and deed.

Satan visits our family in his ancient disguise,
Our love for God and our ways are despised.
He will sow discord and flame our emotions,
He will tear us apart and destroy our devotion.

He lurks in the shadows of each congregation,
He wishes to defile God's sacred foundations.
The father or rumors, the grim reaper of souls,
The strong saints will stand and others will fold.

The tongue of deception makes some fall away,
The family will be tempted to each other betray.
All of the brethren will be lured to dissension,
We all look to our father for hope and redemption.

We must prefer calm while rejecting the storm,
Wise that our adversary takes on many forms.
If we stand as a family holding each other near,
Then all of God's children have nothing to fear.

RENDEZVOUS

I have had my moments of peace and glad grace
Waiting here inside this flesh to see God's holy face.
This body is unaware of the soul it cannot contain
A rendezvous is certain when Jesus calls my name.

In the twinkling of an eye my former self shall rise
I will rise to meet my savior to live and never die.
My remains will reunite for God this plan has made
I will not remain a lofty dust nor hidden in a grave.

One last journey to complete immortal I shall be
As the Lord of all creation is there to welcome me.
A mirror of his reflection no longer held in place
Gravity cannot hold my form its left without a trace.

The death of all the living shall finally be destroyed
The father of all evil things his power null and void.
The king of sin and darkness will burn forever more
A victory cry from heaven love's finally won the war.

"Hell is a reality seen too late." ~ Mark Anthony Grubb

THE MAN I MIGHT HAVE BEEN

Beyond this thing that we call time,
A young child calls to me.
The lad who lived in yesterday,
The boy I use to be.

He comes to me in youthful form,
And tells me I'm his fate.
The tiny boy with tender heart,
Who had not learned to hate.

I showed him all my earthly things,
My goals had met their needs.
He whispered you have missed it all,
Because of all your greed.

I showed him jewels and money,
That I had always craved.
He sighed it can't go with you,
When you go to your grave.

He waved good-bye with tear stained face,
And vanished in the wind.
I cried to think that precious boy,
Was the man I might have been.

FALLEN LEAVES

The leaves have all fallen down
And lie upon the ground.
They fell from lofty perches,
Some didn't make a sound.

The blowing wind has torn them
From the branches of their birth.
Now flying make their journey
To the womb of Mother Earth.

And now they lie here lifeless,
Their bright colors now fade to tan.
It occurred to me at that moment,
How like fallen leaves, is man.

We're born upon this planet;
We come in green and grand.
We come in different colors,
And born in different lands.

We hang upon the tree of life,
As the wind of time blows.
With seasons change our colors
And die when we are old.

THE LEGEND OF THE WEEPING WILLOW

The author prevailing and restless winds,
Speaks to this mortal of weeping limbs.
A forsaken legend in time's been hushed,
A time when a trees heart was touched.

The willow stood straight and would not bend,
But then its foliage was changed by men.
One day when leaves were beginning their change,
The willow saw something new and strange.

In the distance a violent crowd emerged,
Their angry shouts deafened singing birds.
And over his majestic branch was flung,
A rope from which a man was hung.

The man struggled then gave up the ghost,
As the willow sagged to its violent hosts.
The willow wept over the innocent life,
Cursing the men for their blinded strife.

On that autumn day when winds were cold,
At the willows base was laid a soul.
And forever he bows so you will remember,
A murderous day in a timeless November.

I AM GRATEFUL

I am so grateful for men who still weep,
For the faithful shepherd still keeping his sheep.
For the mystical hymns of crickets and doves,
And for gray haired mothers and their labors of love.

I am so grateful for my warm and cozy bed,
And for the prayer of forgiveness that speaks in my head.
For the laughter of children and the spirit that sings,
And for the rebirth and promise and coming of spring.

I am so grateful for the humble knees that still bough,
And for the proud farmer that continues to plow.
For the joy of lovers that believe love is not vain,
And for those who are meek and live with the pain.

I am so grateful for the wonder of new fallen snow,
And for the preacher who still loves my soul.
For the soft heart of doctors who still mourn at a loss,
And for those who fought battles for us at great cost.

I am so grateful for valleys, mountains and peaks,
And for the spirit of courage and the flesh that is weak.
For the faith and the hope I've embraced in my strife,
And for the people I've loved in this marvelous life.

I NEVER TOLD BROTHER

As I ponder my days when I was a boy,
How being with brother was my pride and joy.
I guess I never told him, cause I was ashamed,
Besides I was just a kid with growing pains.

I guess I never told him, he was the best,
Grateful he was family and how I felt blessed.
I never told him in those days young and wild,
That he filled the void of this fatherless child.

I guess I never told him, how it felt inside,
When I walked in his shadow and by his side.
How he was my hero in all of life's games,
I never told brother, so I'll take the blame.

I guess I never told him how bad it hurt,
To wear hand me downs and ragged old shirts.
He must have been tall then cause he couldn't see
Having a brother like him, made a difference to me.

DENIAL

Our lives are written by actions and deeds
With ink we write it then we plant our seeds.
With strokes of indelible ink our words we fit
And human tears won't erase one blot of it.
Choosing our pathways named anger and rage
It's mankind's rebellion just turning a page.
Lives that are fashioned by struggle and strife
Adoring the worldly while denying their life.
Resisting and boastful full of passion and pride
Never admitting that Jesus has suffered and died.

"Life is like listening to a song. You don't understand its true meaning until it's almost over." ~ Mark Anthony Grubb

INVISIBLE PATHS

There are invisible paths that none of us know
It is the paths we trod when we become a soul.
When the final breath is drawn and life is done,
Last chances are finished the race has been run.

Just as geese fly crying overhead so shall it be
As we also follow an invisible path to eternity.
This path was chosen by the way that we lived
So love one another and give it all you can give.

While clocks are still ticking do all that you can
To spread the good news to your fellow man.
Give hope to those in prison do all you can do
Souls hang in the balance so it's all up to you.

Orphans go roaming seeking shelter and heat
No coat on their backs, nor shoes on their feet.
Walk in the paths that the homeless have trod
Look at the poor and you are looking at God.

The lost and the wayward that need your love
Are precious to God who looks on from above.
Don't look away from the suffering and pain
Don't forget the blind, the cripple and lame.

The cry of the widows are heard in the night
Tend to their needs turn the darkness to light.
Bereaved ones need a tender word of cheer
Give all your love wipe away all their tears.

Change the direction of your souls final flight
Do the will of the father with all of your might.
Every face that we see each day of our life
Is a lamb that belongs to the Lord Jesus Christ.

BIBLE OF ROSES

I pondered the days on which these
Roses were so neatly tucked away.
Now buried in this Bible as a
Memory of sad and mournful days.

Who had plucked these single roses
From their sweet beloved's bed?
As I read the front inscription it
Was mother's words I read.

To whom would read this Bible
I have kept throughout the years.
Will find it full of roses
And pages stained with tears.

Each rose represents a living soul
Now gone from this sad time.
The tear stained pages are my own
As I read each verse and line.

The roses you see withered here
Now bloom in glories sod.
For just like me they are reborn
And now abide with God.

BRIEF EXPLANATIONS

Life is brief
Night falls still.
Flesh is weak
Spirit has will.

Yesterday is done
Today will fade.
Tomorrow is distant
Times slipping away.

Tears fall silent
Smiles spreading wide.
Anger strikes quickly
Shadows cannot hide.

The soul is joyful
God never lies.
Hearts still beating
Love never dies.

SOUL SURVIVORS

An enchanted existence inside of our heads,
Suspended entrapment not living nor dead.
We're frozen in time without future or past,
Music is all that will make memories last.

The beauty of Eden left us here all alone,
Baptized by God Adam and Eve are gone.
We are soul survivors of all that remains,
Living in the shadows of a perfect domain.

Humanity's sentimental journey never ends,
The beauty of love we've tainted with sin.
Satan's whispers are bolder in evil ways,
As time is running out in these end of days.

We're soul survivors through amazing grace,
Can still live again in God's promised place.
Let us wake up from our reckless slumber,
Singing, "Lord I want to be in that number".

We no longer dwell in a wire tapped garden,
The son of God died and gave us our pardon.
But the price that was paid demands our life
To be one of worship for our lord Jesus Christ.

THE PROMISE

I see traces of life in the ground below
And bare branches sprout buds that grow.
The birds that vanished have reappeared
Singing their love songs I've waited to hear.

The air is moving with those moving things
The ones God made that move upon wings.
The noise of insects that slept in the ground
Fill both day and night with musical sounds.

Everything is alive with the coming of spring
We see the beauty of God's marvelous things.
The season of resurrection has finally arrived
The promise of rebirth to all things that died.

PHENOMENON

Our existence on this tiny planet,
As we travel in time and space.
We are God's living phenomenon,
We're called the human race.

Souls evolve to thinking flesh,
That strain on simple words.
We ride upon these molecules
Where blood and spirit merge.

A thinking soul that questions,
Contemplating the who of me.
Both solid form and vapor,
A phenomenon of reality.

The brainchild and the family
The creation God called man.
A swirling mist of emotions,
Formed by God's own hands.

Phenomenon of all creation
God's love had took a shape.
The union of man and woman,
With power to chose their fate.

The envy of all hosts in heaven
The angels look on and rejoice.
Freewill living with a purpose
A soul with a heart and a voice.

THE MASTERPIECE

I had looked at many pictures that life had drew for me,
Some were drawn with happiness and some with agony.
Portraits of this earthly journey and how I made my run,
Centered around the masterpiece of God's beloved son.

Immoral men and women so unashamed and lightly clad,
Sick with sin and minds defiled and now they all are mad.
The power of the light that shines on each and every face,
Is the God of all creation that offers his redeeming grace.

Poses froze within a frame, a smile with laughing eyes,
Pictures of pure innocence and sweet lips that never lie.
A rugged cross and mocking crowds adorns my gallery,
Blood and tears all point the way to a hill called Calvary.

Among so many pictures that were drawn by mortal man
Well trained eyes can see the one that had the master plan.
Another picture centered that hangs with crimson blood,
The sacrifice of Jesus the masterpiece of God's own love.

"As a society we are having a serious identity crisis. We've forgotten who God is therefore we have no clue as to who we are anymore." ~ Mark Anthony Grubb

AND GOD CREATED DOGS

God created dogs to fill the breech,
A human need no man could reach.
The chemistry we don't understand,
The bond between a dog and man.

Their eyes search ours for one clue
What could it be that pleases you?
Keen awareness they sense disaster,
Protect their love who is their master.

Your wish is always their command,
How special is this bond with man?
No pretense in their own emotions,
And wagging tails are joy in motion.

Barking greetings when we arrive,
So glad we're home and we're alive.
Devoted friend unconditional love,
Could only be created by God above.

THE FIRST TIME

One bolt across the horizon,
One chance for me to say.
To get it right the first time,
To live and give God's way.

An image with a conscience,
A clay that's special made.
Creation in a flash of light,
That soon begins to fade.

A gasp of contemplation,
Is all that I can give.
The genie in this bottle
Comes out one time to live.

A single wandering heart,
One chance to ride the wind.
To get it right the first time,
To purge this soul of sin.

THE DEVIL COMES TO PLAY

A thought that is forbidden
An unkind thought or deed.
It's Satan playing tag again
His demons planting seeds.

Our mind is his playground
He knows our turf so well.
He beckons us to follow
His path that leads to hell.

The mortal soul is his prey
He baits Jehovahs lambs.
Temptation is not limited
He taunts the great I am.

The sandbox is a favorite
The serpents box of toys.
He lures us with his candy
And then he takes our joy.

He loves to play the doctor
With black bag in his hand.
He then quickly opens it
To shed disease on man.

He is old death incarnate
Grim reaper riding fast.
Time is swiftly moving
He knows it will not last.

Beware of his playground
He always comes to play.
Climb in the arms of Jesus
And never leave nor stray.

THE SEA OF LIFE

Sometimes we steer a crooked course
And our wind is self-esteem.
A journey through this world called life
As we live to the extreme.

We're sailing across an ocean wide
Like voyagers roaming free.
Interrupted by life's violent storms
Upon these restless seas.

Searching for a lighthouse beacon
As the storm lashes out with might.
Looking for one faint light of hope
Our sanctuary nowhere in sight.

The winds of change are blowing
No peace within this gale.
No land in sight nor friendly port
But onward yet we sail.

Souls drifting on these waves
Are easily tossed about.
The darkness of these waters
Leaves us full of doubt

We seek mercy from the master
A word from his command.
He will surely show the way
And guide us safe to land.

VACANCY

Dreams turn to ashes and now our body's cold,
Our arms locked forever with nothing left to hold.
Lips that are unmoving and hearts are very still,
Death has left us lifeless and it has took our will.

This body is not forever its only flesh and bones
It will long to stay here but earth is not our home.
The soul that dwells inside us it lingers patiently,
For death to claim our bodies and leave a vacancy.

His holy seed incarnate with endless aching needs,
To gratify our body that leaves our souls to bleed.
Mortal human beings in whom God has left his mark,
Children of the almighty God but yet we fear the dark.

Shadows of God's image who cannot understand,
The plan nor the purpose of why God created man.
Of all that he created it is we who were special made
A living immortal soul that will not die within a grave.

SUSPENDED BY WOOD

Tiny baby's feet and hands that rest on hay
Pierced with nails on our redemption day.
Can you imagine his back scourged and beat?
And a crown of thorns and nail scarred feet.

How could men spit upon this innocent face
Who is the creator of all and the human race?
How swaddling clothes would be stripped away
To humiliate our God on his last human day?

In this bed of hay lays the epitome of love
Sweet baby eyes soon filled with blood.
Small baby lips that grin and upwards curl
Soon beg for mercy for a sin sick world.

This helpless child grows to humble man
But remains God of all and the great I am.
This child so lowly no crib for his bed
Born in a trough where cattle are fed.

Born of a virgin and in a cradle was laid
Wood was the sign of a price to be paid.
At birth and at death it was Jesus that would
Be born and die cradled by some form of wood.

He's coming back soon are you ready or lost?
Your redemption is free and there isn't a cost.
Yet the cost that he paid for you and for me
Was born in a manger and died on a tree.

I WON'T RECALL

As I ponder my mortality
I think of my rebirth.
My spirit that awakens
When I depart this earth.

I won't recall our time dear
My soul will find release.
And travel on to paradise
Where I shall find my peace.

All former things will pass away
No need for carnal pleasure.
No ticking clocks marking time
No days nor years to measure.

My end of time came quickly
My beating heart fell still.
I don't recall one memory
Nor have a human will.

Changing in an instant
My spirit starts to glow.
But I will not remember
What's going on below.

Recall the time God gave us
Before I had to go.
So I won't die inside your heart
As you grow gray and old.

THE LIVING WORD

The spirits seed clothed in flesh
When God came to Bethlehem.
His own image in all creation
Was the one that he called man.

He felt the earth below his feet
He hungered and he thirst.
He felt every emotion in every
Human alive upon the earth.

He saw us die and saw disease
Faith spared some now and then.
He saw the chaos Satan caused
With his death and all the sin.

He left his home in heaven
In Mary's womb he was made.
He came to live and die for us
From the cradle to the grave.

So he shared his living word
It spread both far and wide.
Then they came and took him
They flogged and crucified.

The living word fell silent
With lips so parched and dry.
All his sheep were scattered
And no light was in the sky.

The ground it shook in anger
He hung there all alone.
His people who called him king
Had nailed him to his throne.

"You can't see forever from here but you can feel it."
~ Mark Anthony Grubb

THE PRICE OF TIME

Mirrors reflect reality of our face,
Youth has vanished without a trace.
Our stage where beauty appeared,
Is now covered by tracks of tears.
Minds become cloudy and we are frail,
Youthful skin becomes weak and pale.
Our voice changes and nothing's clear,
When we're aging and cannot hear.
Our clothes of flesh are not the same,
Legs of youth need walkers and canes.
Our sharp vision has faded from view,
Our list of friends grows to just a few.
Hollow eyes and highways of lines,
Are payments for the price of time.
Time will bend our backs and knees,
Pride reduced to prayers and pleas.

WHO WILL FOLD THE FLAG FOR YOU

Our flag so brave in battle
It's red with crimson blood.
It shows the sign of struggle
Been burned and thrown in mud.

She's flown over many places
Where men and women died.
The flag was folded for them
As loved ones watched and cried.

The flag bows down with honor
As one lonely trumpet plays.
Taps is sounding its farewell
As to eternal rest they're laid.

Hero's that we dare not forget
Sons and daughters we have lost.
As the flag is folded for them
For the ones that paid the cost.

This is the price of freedom
The red, the white, the blue.
The best of what we stand for
Who will fold the flag for you?

HEART TO HEART

From heaven to heaven your power you weave,
God of all creation my first love you're my majesty.
The power of your love showered on we the lost,
Things we endear here count all things but loss.

You have created the seasons for the benefit of man,
Oceans alive with your thoughts and mountains to span.
More than anything you created man so special and apart,
From the beginning he was the creation from your heart.

You hung stars and planets for the love of man to see,
All placed so man could look out in the eye of eternity.
Intelligence was spawn into a living brain of notions,
A piece of your heart filled with all of your emotions.

Heart to heart we are born coupled to the great I am,
Father son and Holy Ghost, Emmanuel, the word and lamb.
The lamb and Lion of Judah the rage and the peace of calm,
Fire of salvation, still waters of the soul, our song of psalm.

FADE AWAY

Flower children begin to slowly fade away,
The generation of the love child and JFK.
Protestors of war and the creators of song,
All of yesterday's hippies are almost gone.

Soldiers scarred by war came back alone,
In flag covered coffins they're finally home.
No parades or fanfare were ever planned,
For youth who gave it all on foreign land.

Mayberry was the place where we could go,
Where we felt safe and life could really flow.
No news from Hanoi and the tallies of life,
Gut wrenching scenes that cut like a knife.

History repeats the saga of north and south,
As her pages show war is not the way out.
Selective service and bingo a bloody game,
Left mothers crying and a nation in shame.

Landing on the moon was our nation's pride,
But her sons and daughters continued to die.
The pill and the Beatles were the latest craze,
Peace was the drum beat back in those days.

Now finding peace when it was always there,
Reading King James in their rocking chairs.
Christ is the way now and a new hope is here,
The new chant has changed to faith over fear.

THE MIST

I inhaled my soul as I took my first breath,
A miracle with the rise and fall of my chest.
My spirit and I both share the same space,
The image of God is here etched on my face.

Father God had many expectations from me,
From the very first day that I came to be.
But freedom tempted me to seek other ways,
While Satan tempted this new house of clay.

I haunted my soul looking for something else,
When all I needed to find was God and myself.
I found them waiting for their lost prodigal son,
Deep inside my mist from whence I had come.

I saw multitudes of reflections all over the place
In the mirror of forever I saw everyone's face.
My God, my savior and the holy spirit all in one,
Cleansed me and forgave me for all I had done.

"Silence is a symphony that plays within our minds, the chords of every thought and word that's lived throughout all time." ~ Mark Anthony Grubb

PEACE ON THE WING

The dull grey birds approached the fields,
To search out seeds and have their fill.
The whistling of air they always bring,
God's symbols of peace are on the wing.

Some relatives wait on nearby post,
Eyes reflecting the sky of approaching host.
Then silence is shattered by roaring sounds,
As feathered limp bodies fall to the ground.

These shots that raged from shotgun bores,
Stopped tiny hearts beating forevermore.
On nearby ground cuddled breast to breast,
The sad mournful doves find eternal rest.

I cradled one bird as distant cattle cried,
Rude red marks displays how it had died.
I thought how God had used the Dove,
To symbolize peace and the power of love.

How can we plead for peace on earth?
Being hypocrites of love and living worth.
Liberators of perversion swiping cobweb dreams,
Predators stalking peace that's on the wing.

BEYOND MY BLINDNESS

Beyond my blindness and power to see,
A real existence is waiting and calling to me.
A world full of beauty anointed with love,
A sky full of mysteries that dwell up above.

In nature there lies many gifts and pleasures,
Creations God gave us to nurture and treasure.
It is beyond my grasp, to behold all there is,
To comprehend the universe is alive and it lives.

Beyond my vision and many light years away,
A galaxy is affected by things that I say.
For I am one unit in the motion and flow,
In a sea of creation that continues to grow.

In the eye of the universe a tear is found,
For each bird and star that falls to the ground.
One aware of the other, the birth and the fall,
Their existence now finished and can't be recalled.

Beyond my revelations and the wisdom of years,
A bright star is born while a new rose appears.
A real existence is waiting and calling to me,
But I remain blind and I cannot see.

MIDNIGHT PERFORMANCE

Sleep will not impart its peace
To this foolish heart of mine.
As eyes of sand, their vigil keep
Of worlds somewhere in time.

Observing frolic of the bats
Like sleds on ice bound hills.
Night gives way to prowling cats
In search of their next kill.

Flutter of wings in silver sky
The Nighthawk dives through space.
Silence yields to one shrill cry
As his eyes on quarry trace.

I hear the distant barking dog
In the distant forest deep.
I hear frogs sing in nearby bog
Where bugs become the feast.

Its midnight and the story
Within its archives deep,
That I observe this glory
On nights I cannot sleep.

MILLERS POND

My brother and I took a trip into yesterday,
Our archives of youth and places we played.
Then we drove back to old Millers Pond,
A place where our souls had woven a bond.

As we looked upon her we recalled old stories,
And we lost our breath just beholding her glory.
We saw the shadows of brothers holding hands,
A time when we were in love with this land.

Her waters move slower just like brother and I,
As we remember her beauty of days now gone by.
We saw ourselves lying on banks slick and worn,
The soil from which family memories were born.

We looked on the waters and things became clearer,
The pond had reflections of life's viewing mirror.
The pond's grown old and time has taken its toll,
On two young boys with wood fishing poles.

We experienced time travel both pure and pleasant,
But time demanded we return to the present.
As we glanced back two ghostly figures remained,
Two young boys fishing with poles made of cane.

THE SAND DOLLAR

Abandoned by the lashing foam
Laid still upon the beach.
One sole Sand Dollar lies
Alone forsaken by the deep.

As sea gull calls subsided,
I wondered if it heard.
The ebbing tide as music
And pounding waves as words.

This coin of Neptune's kingdom
I pondered what it felt.
As cold death is approaching,
Its harsh embrace is felt.

This sad time of departing
Unites all things with man.
All living things will crumble,
At touch return to sand.

Aged urchin just like man
Will grieve the fading tide.
And in the final moments,
Will yearn to be alive.

SCHOOL SPIRITS

Dedicated to John S. Battle High School

We who were here for a moment in time,
Still roam these halls within our minds.
We are the spirit of the Trojan song,
This place we haunt and for it long.

We are the roots from whence you came,
Times have changed but we're still the same.
Time can only fracture and makes us old,
It can't destroy dreams or kill the soul.

This school that's full of youthful sounds,
Is our alma mater and hallowed ground.
Here we school spirits laugh and play,
Your time to join us is a heartbeat away.

In our time we all loved this place,
Enjoy your stay, because it's getting late.
Cherish the laughter be grateful for friends,
For youth disappears like dust in the wind.

TIME IS ON THE WING

In these times to God we cling,
Time is passing it's on the wing.
Do the things that you must do,
The signs are here and on the news.

You will perish if you're not saved
So heed God's word & just obey.
He loves you & mere words can't say,
He shed his blood your debt is paid.

The end of days are here right now
The time when every knee shall bow.
Babe of Bethlehem has become our King,
Time is fading and it's on the wing.

IF I COULD FLY

As long as I can remember I've wanted to fly,
And soar among eagles in cloud covered skies.
Go across the horizon and beyond mountain peaks,
And play upon rainbows their colors I'd sweep.

Upwards I'd surge above valleys and steams,
Streaking through space to its outer extremes.
Escape all this gravity that has held me in place,
Disappear among stars without a clue or a trace.

I'd skip over moonbeams and hurl them like toys,
The comets would race me with laughter and joy.
I'd converse with Antares about vision and sight,
In the stillness of space I would hum Silent Night.

I'd look upon Saturn and the rings she adorns,
And peek upon places where planets are born.
With the wind to my back to heaven I'd fly,
And there play with angels and with them abide.

"Wrinkles are the shadows of the footprints of time determined by the measure of grief, joy and love in our lifetime." ~ Mark Anthony Grubb

LOVE FOUND A WAY

I was crucified on Calvary's hill,
It was the plan and my father's will.
The cost of sin was mine to pay,
My father's love had found a way.

Hanging there I saw your face,
And every soul in the human race.
I recalled that day when I was born
How I was loved on Christmas morn.

Son of man turning thirty three
Was born to die upon this tree.
I felt your pain and all your strife,
I surrendered all and gave my life.

The sky turned dark as angels cried
I tasted death, but I did not die.
I did God's will and did obey
My father's love had found a way.

CHILDREN OF THE STORM

God moves in mysterious ways
His miracles he performs.
He made footsteps on the sea
And calmed the angry storm.

The father of his children's minds
All blessed with special skills.
We sing the songs of victory
And do his sovereign will.

As children do we go astray
As blind when we were born.
God sees us lost and helpless
And saves us from the storm.

We praise the rose of Sharon
The son of man is born.
To rescue all who seek him
And save us from the storm.

BORROWED BODY

I do not recall my arrival upon this splendid earth,
Nor my cries of sadness when mother gave me birth.
I came here weak and helpless just a fragile babe,
Born in a borrowed body that lasts me to the grave.

Flesh created by the union of a woman and a man
Mortal and immortality the brain child of God's plan.
The envy of the angels that behold the fathers face
Human in appearance but a soul redeemed by grace.

A borrowed body born that strains on simple words
A heart full of emotion where blood and spirit merge.
A complex combination I'm least but still I'm most,
A simple human being both flesh and living ghost.

Satan is no stranger to this dust from Adam's seed,
Beloved son named Jesus has died to set me free.
I'm part of all that's living the clay in the potter's hand
The image of my father I'm the reason, I am man.

IF ALL WE HAD WAS US

The world is void and empty
To those who bear the cross.
Despised for loving Jesus
By those who are still lost.

Christians lean on Jesus
For strength in every day.
For if we forge alone you see
We'd soon forget our way.

Knowing God is with us
Our guide on paths unknown.
The cross the only shadow
For we who walk alone.

Faith is so important
In our God we surely trust.
Just imagine how alone we'd be
If all we had was us.

HOW COULD WE KNOW

Dedicated to the Victims of Sandy Hook Elementary School

The last supper done and tucked in their beds
The last time the pillow would cuddle their heads.
A last glance at the tree, the presents and bows,
Their gifts never opened but how could we know?

Tiny hands were washed and breakfast was served
And thanks be to God was the last prayer they heard.
The last trip to school full of laughter and cheers,
Would all end abruptly with screams and with tears.

Swings now hang lonely and pets stare at the place
Looking for the arrival of their friends smiling face.
Unique little voices that filled playgrounds with joy
Won't sing Jingle Bells or play with their toys.

How could we know this was their homecoming day?
Hasten by men's hatred that would take them away.
God's innocent souls that we all loved and adored
Would never leave school or come home anymore.

THE STREET NAMED FOREVER

I'm standing by in paradise
As the Lord prepares for me.
A mansion he has promised
And it I soon will see.

My mansion is very special
It's not rooted in the ground.
It stands up there in glory
And I am heaven bound.

It's part of a golden city
The carpenter is the lamb.
This is divine construction
Built by nail scarred hands.

My neighbors will be angels
They're all amazed at man.
Flesh redeemed by Jesus
The masterpiece of the plan.

Death cannot enter there
And tears are not allowed.
My street name is forever
My front porch is the clouds.

SIX HOURS TO PARADISE

This man named Jesus who walked the sea
He healed the sick and made the blind to see.
He cast out demons and hushed the storm
This was the purpose for which he was born.

He turned water to wine and raised the dead
We were saved and healed by words he said.
The word became flesh yet spoke not a word
When asked for his plea nothing was heard.

His vision became blurred by a crown of thorns
Blood running down where his flesh was torn.
His parched lips begged God to forgive all men
To forgive those who crucified of all their sins.

He could have called ten thousand angels down
But he spoke not a word nor uttered a sound.
When the nails were driven into Jesus hands
They pierced creation and the creator of man.

In his final moments while here on this earth
He recalled his short journey and even his birth.
His life in the flesh over and all prophecy fulfilled
Death had been conquered by doing God's will.

THE SONG

I am the song that needs a voice,
I am a hymn that makes you rejoice.
I am the beauty when you dream,
Sad and glad and in between.

The sun when you are feeling cold,
The song of youth when you are old.
I am the mood that makes you dance,
I am the words of pure romance.

I am the song that makes you bow
The whistling farmer behind the plow.
I am the melody that knows no fear
I am the song that you need to hear.

I am the lullaby that rocks the babe,
The shout of victory in your grave.
I am the chord that makes you cry,
I am the song sung when you die.

I am the seven wonders of the world,
I am the song between a boy and girl.
I am the miracle that makes you sing,
The proof that God lives in everything.

"When the taunt strings of life fall invisibly to my sides my soul shall raise up and I will shout with a new voice the victory cry over death." ~ Mark Anthony Grubb

DID YOU EVER LAUGH?

A man of many sorrows,
Our Lord while here was known.
He spoke to crowds and masses,
Yet prayed and cried alone.

Not a single verse in scripture
Shows laughter in your face.
Perhaps you wept with joy instead
Our lamb of God's own grace.

Did the weight of our sins Lord
Take your laughter all away?
Was your heart heavy burdened
By things you heard men say?

Did you ever laugh dear Jesus
When you were just a babe?
Or was your laughter stifled
By a world of souls to save?

NEMESIS

We are searching for direction in every waking hour,
The battle of good and evil both have decisive power.
Which will be the victor is the eternal question asked,
The answer is in the present not the future or the past.

Satan sends his demons to tempt and take control,
This Nemesis of corruption that seeks our mortal souls.
The best at mass deception a harbinger of empty lies,
Power hungry leaders that watch their countries die.

The masquerade unending he taunts and intercedes,
Perverting truth and justice is how he plants his seeds.
False prophet of the ages this light from heaven fell,
The master of all misery in evil hearts does dwell.

Footfalls sound like thunder as men and women fall,
The voice of Eden's liar who lures them with his call.
The road to hell is paved with bleaching bones of saints,
Who yielded to their Nemesis and didn't show restraint.

A LOOK INSIDE

Though our lives encounter strife
Love is all that matters in this life.
When we see others deep within
We see past hate and all the sin.

When we see inside we see the pain
And the fact our lives are not in vain.
... We see the tears that cloud the eye
We will see the soul that never dies.

We will not see the color of the skin
We'll see the place where it all begin.
We will see more than flesh and bone
We will see that we are never alone.

We'll see a glow with an unseen source
We'll see a path with a charted course.
We will see that faith has held us close
That we are carnal and living ghost.

You will see the DNA of our God on high
Nail scarred hands and a pierced side.
You will see things quite different and new
You will see all of creation is created in you.

THE PROMISE

I see traces of life in the ground below
And bare branches sprout buds that grow.
The birds that vanished have reappeared
Singing their love songs I've waited to hear.

The air is moving with those moving things
The ones God made that move upon wings.
The noise of insects that slept in the ground
Fill both day and night with musical sounds.

Everything is alive with the coming of spring
We see the beauty of God's marvelous things.
The season of resurrection has finally arrived
The promise of rebirth to all things that died.

THE TRESPASSER

Adam and Eve were happy tending the green garden of life called earth, when suddenly a falling star streaked across the heavens and from the star emerged a lowly trespasser. The sly serpent slithered about paradise planning and plotting. The father of darkness had come calling on the beauty of creation with his vile and calculated ways. He planned the moment he would strike sinking his fangs deep into the flesh of immortality putting an end to man and fouling God's own plan. As Adam and Eve ate their fate a chilling victory cry from death shook the heavens and in return a battle cry from God's archangels was quickly hushed. Satan shuddered as the shadow of a cross reflected on the rivers of life and in the far distance a faint cry of a single lamb was heard in the silence of space.

JUST FOR ME

A soul survivor without a name,
Born into flesh that feels the pain.
A falling star lighting up the sky,
Arriving shouting one lonely cry.

Life was a flash and one breath,
Flesh that soon is taken by death.
We question what life is about,
So many paths, just two routes.

Food controlled by sun and rain,
Life is a cycle of constant change.
Wind that dances with the trees,
God made them all just for me.

He sent me love from the start,
Isn't it a pity how we drift apart?
I am part of all I touch and see,
Amazing grace made just for me.

BONE BY BONE

I'm not a hollow shell I thought
I'm not just here by chance.
You built me bone by bone
Oh Lord to do a special dance.

A life of purpose is my goal
It burns within my soul.
You didn't simply place me
Here to die when I am old.

My soul joins a single cell
On earth in mother's womb.
Awaken from another place
To come to earth to bloom.

Time's clock started ticking
I emerge with baby's cry.
My soul had now awaken
First thought was I'm alive.

Homesick for my image
That God had promised me.
Both flesh and living soul
Combined God set me free.

Free to live and breathe
Make choices in this form.
I alone decide my destiny
Seeking shelter in the storm.

Time is not without an end
And earth is not my home.
Jesus is the king of kings
And sits upon his throne.

And I must do his will
Before my soul ascends.
Bone by bone I fail and fall
Until life's journey ends.